Velleity's Shade

T0160066

saturnalia books

Velleity's Shade

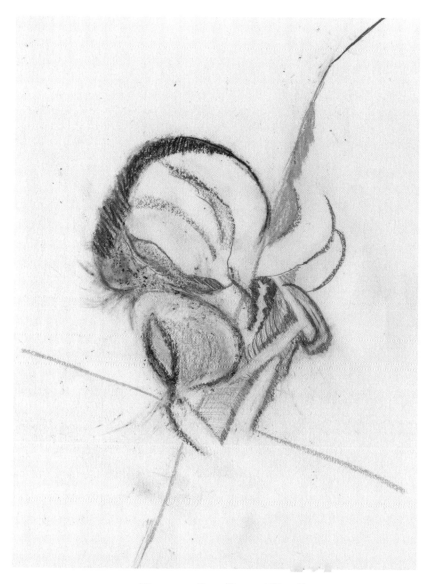

Poetry by Star Black

Paintings by Bill Knott

Artist/Poet Collaboration Series Number Six

Saturnalia Books
Ardmore, PA 19003
info@saturnaliabooks.com

ISBN: 978-0-9818591-7-
Library of Congress Control Number: 2010934204

Book Design by Saturnalia Books
Printing by Westcan Printing Group, Canada

Cover Art: Slice Missing on Left, mixed media on canvas, 2007
Back Cover: The Cineastes, mixed media on paper, 2006
Title Page: Hammerflower, mixed media on paper, 200?

Distributed by:
University Press of New England
1 Court Street
Lebanon, NH 03766
800-421-1561

The author gratefully acknowledges the following publications in which some of these poems first appeared: *The Awl* (online), *Barrow Street*, *The Best American Poetry Blog* (online), *The Paris Review*, *The Southampton Review*, *Parnassus*, *Ploughshares*, and *Sous Rature* (online).

Table of Contents

Titles of Paintings

Velleity's Shade

APOLOGIA

I've been reading the beginning of "D"—
dbb, daguerrean, dairymaid, dawk lost
in a datamation of thought, intrigued
by Scottish slang and Greek daughters

(obedient Danaides condemned to sieve
water in Hades) and I need to tell you
our relationship is exhausting; we can be
one and one, not two, and we have tried

everything but compromise which is,
of course, too unenlightening and no fun.
Meanwhile, we edge toward demise,
dust-mop-like, courteous, respectful,

hoping to avoid a new life, its droll shock,
yet I adore you; dawdling, I'm caught.

SEASONAL

Behind the deep-brown evening gowns
of last year's Oscars, the shadows of deer
pervade the dim-lit roads. They are everywhere,
starved from recesses by gated estates

as near-miss spectres in the iridescent,
midnight gloam, They must be either fed or shot,
depending upon the town committee. Flowerbeds
are at risk, and flowers have immunity,

whereas deer are "thinned" and, yet,
Bjork's swan dress will never end; years
will retrieve that red-carpet splash, the smile
so innocent, so fashion-savvy. Style's

a weird category: what stays, what goes—
the taste of venison, a taste for clothes.

SOAKED

Sleeping at night with various kings,
banquets rolling from wooden bowls,
chalices flipped, did she surmise
an overcast to those lapsed

evenings in her morning bath?
Or were the moments too magical,
too bannered? And what of the future,
the recent past, did they exist

in scented water, the bacchanals
over, the castle mute? She never asked,
she never wandered. The water surrounded
her and, then, everything began

in a stark fuzz. Contact
was banter, banter was love.

NOON

I wish I were Aphra Behn
and could comply with wicked men
and feast on momentary fire,
laughing as the embers tire,

randomizing masked desire
without an oath or least remorse
for the splutterwheels of force
that trump the rumpled mire.

I'd give the flowered Geishas skies
the color of a bitten plum
and make bereft aubades all lies
as I'd prefer the sun,

but Aphra Behn is very dead
as is this instant and the bed.

LOST TREE OF HEAVEN

The weedy ailanthus tree is curious,
like Rossetti's lily in The Annunciation, thirst-
thin, the dolled Virgin recoiling, frightened
of the glorious stem. Its highest leaves

rise and rise from roots that thrive
in the most inhospitable conditions—under
jagged stones, in disordered courtyards,
between brownstones, in sleet or

shade, without care or notice—yet
the weed-tree's solace of green muslin
makes any window prosperous in a city
where so many trees die of disease,

so when it dies, everything green dies;
windows face windows, all day, all night.

DARK-HAIRED DAWNS

Like a girl Ted Bundy found sleeping, I feel
fatally small. Hiroshima, Nagasaki, is that all?
Are we finally diminished? May we hip-hop
back to space in Whitey-Ford innings?

It was clear as a bell on the moon,
'ere derivatives and bundled loans, 'ere
accountability and Slim Pickens' windmills.
The moon was free, the moon was ours.

Everybody loves the moon. How
many C.S.I.s must we see to fly there soon
like a green billionaire, and will we hear
the doves coo in a spatial memory,

doves trapped by vendors so Buddhists
can pay to set them free, free of me, of Bundy?

THE DREAM OF TAP WATER

A spare apartment, a Shaker interior,
a Spartan sofa, and a cat named Hysteria,
make a career feel at home, if inferior,
bound to a room without a shadow.

Does the hat rack spin? Are the hats
compatible? The cushions coordinated,
correctly couched? Or is one dismissive
of plaids and argyles, and would prefer

to own a house? What of the window-
washers? Will they survive the scaffold's
heights, the squeegeed weather that almost
rattles with what most perceive as daylight?

It seems sad to think that things are
never altogether right, but complaining
to the super is dicey, especially after midnight.

TWILIT

Moving away from rattled towns,
gaining, as a bird in a dishwasher,
an altered view, the owlish lakefronts
with their punch-clock crews

seem less luckless, the lunch-pail
chatter less dim; even recess seems pleasant.
Schoolmates from the third grade call
and nothing since matters,

you leap into kerosene waters
and swim, leaving the nervous talons
on a perch. The past doesn't hurt,
the past is divine, everyone

the same age at the same time.
Moving is a white lie, a soft arrow.

LOVE IS BONKERS

Why are you so obsessed with Janus?
Why do you look both ways at once while
I'm right here, in home-run proximity,
stalled in a fender-bender fuss?

You're moody, you're slippery, you're
to no avail. You're a snarling improbability
in a second-hand coat, trudging through snow
between the bank and the library, like a

a bookie betting on the next sky to sink
behind the enemy before it retrenches for a new
attack, and, then, suddenly, you're Brad Pitt

in a skirt, urging the inert through doors
of perception until hinges hurt, giving everyone
a free pass at least once, making luck fair.

EFFORT'S ALIBI

Isn't November enough already?
Haven't we said it all? There is nothing
between us but a hyped scrawl. Are we trying
to be a Christmas pretzel? Trying to

scatter school notes on the floor
as glyphs for a janitor to unscramble
on the night shift? Haven't we been here
a thousand times before and gotten—

zip—nowhere? We're nailed to a chair
as zombies enthralled by Metallica. We've
out-Gothed what love suggests: intimacy
in direct proportion to rebellion. You

don't even need me, nor do I, yet we
can't give up the replay, the old college try.

POESY

Red-button issue, the lakes miss you.
The Great Pumpkin season does too, even
if every special feature ever made for
television excludes you, except

those on John Cage and Yoko Ono.
I'm on a bus that never stops stopping
and I'm flipped out. You are the hum
of memory, just so, the Internal

Revenue's alter-ego, my Freudian
slip. Of course, joy doesn't pay much,
too intermittent; foliage is free, the rent isn't,
but look at me on a bus that never

arrives, a spouse who refuses to marry,
a commuter who doesn't drive.

UPGRADE AUBADE

These self-to-self-help interviews
moonshell the wastes as peepshows
the Grim Reaper drinks in at a carnival,
but you just ordered a new computer

with a screen saver of egrets, which
is nice. Their low, white, lifting flights
over deep greens reawaken a compassion
for delicate things, for the soft-spoken,

amber windhovers, and mice. I tried
not to override preliminaries with rhyme
but didn't reach the breakthrough in time
and had to start over. I should have

tried harder, and am. Absolutely.
Hope the new computer comes in handy.

GHOSTED

Boxed and buried in my clothes
with the remnants of a rose and a beauty
mark that's bruised (for as Sir John
Suckling knew "If of herself she

will not love, nothing can make
her") I will have died for probity,
probity and solitude, and Christina Rossetti
will say so. I want a peach rose

and no guests, just Taps blown
by a spook for unassembled filaments
that float and float. (Give biplanes
a rest: they've done enough.)

Vacancy's chanceless, so replete.
I bought a hotdog, crossed the street.

WHITE WHIRL

Indulgent trees, soon stripped by
baptisms in ice, flutter in coup d'oeils
of sacrifice: winter that makes windscapes
so particular like saints in white beards

tortured by famished slaves–who else?–
everyone else is too nice. Pluto would like
this view of the backyard, his status as a planet
downgraded, his dark canopies frayed,

his black lakes, like money, handsomely
made: everything green a silkscreen of black
pomegranate seeds. Knowing him, he'd
come after me, offering dice dots, six,

and, doubling the gift, who can resist?
My mother can, apparently. Tough cookie.

MESSED UP

In our day, the derivative of Bacon's
Pope Innocent X is "anger management"–

an outburst followed by a convoluted story
that makes everyone squeamish who listens.

One sees a Bacon pontiff at every party
but it's best to leave that riveting glare

to an obscure biography. All that time
spent in libraries of forgotten scenes leads

to a stair, ascending and ascending. There,
foibles are unending and who really cares?

I do. The rest is rue. The best are violated
while Innocent X slouches toward Xanadu.

SKY-HOPPING

Girls always hoped squadrons of satyrs
would descend and elope them, carry them
into the forest and tear them open with Pan's
pipe, but they were sent to psychiatrists

to discuss such dreams in private and
then to church to pray history would end,
then to school to study Dali and Dali's friends,
and then to work to obey men. By the time

they got home they were strait-laced and
savvy, determined to update pantheism and get
ahead without rocking the boat as Anita Hill did,
which never works, and to forget Psyche

and ripped nighties, and steal off with Krishna,
his Vedic blue, to dervish the dreamlight.

INSCAPE COMPLAINT

The bouquets went away, miffed
at shoelaces that wrote their initials
in the dust en route to the humor train
that loved children so much it kidnapped
half of them and dropped them off at
zip codes, leaving the playground

ashen, with beagles and chows,
replacements for friendships that last
a New York minute. How did we fall into
this morning-glory instant, its soulful boundaries
turning inward, as if to catch a performance
that never happens, Godot-ago, nada—
and when will we hop a train back

to back again, again, and play
stickball with Solomon and Solomon
Grundy and Solomon Grundy's best friends
and get grubby and make grubby impressions?
It's too late to pretend we belong here,
snug in a heady situation, perfect
enough to let loose the next

balloon and, entangled in a string
hitched to helium, ascend and ascend.

LAND OF UNEASE

I forgive you for everything
you have never done and the rain
does, too. You've never beat me with
a stick, you've never shot me with a gun,
you've neither raped me nor escaped me and

I forgive you, you and I are one,
and I still like your hairdo, the first one,
the one I fell in love with while we were young
and everyone wanted to be an American Indian, an
appellation that no longer exists, that is unforgiven for

good reason.

THE UMBRELLA'S BIO

If we met on the beach to noncommunicate,
if we stopped doodling while thinking,
well, not thinking, exactly, because, if
thinking were appropriate, we'd be surfing
or, at least, wet, but if we could take
noncommunicating seriously and forget
the clammy difficulty of being together,
each insisting upon our own point of view
when your point of view doesn't matter and
my point of view doesn't matter because
we're together on a shore of waves, do you
think, then, things would be less strained?
No, I don't want to go to work today, no, you
don't want to teach. Probably, if we got
down to it, we'd like to noncommunicate.

THE OBLIGING SKY

Shadows collapse in the webwork
of leaves, cooled by squirrels, and huge
old trees, home-insurance liabilities,
felled to protect them from falling,

are stumps. Low, frumpish greens
look surly, half-filched, ragged with crows—
shrubs gnawed by slugs in a dryness that's
decomposed. I've wasted my time

in the spotty sun, loving what's false,
loving the idea of love, its underwhelming
chintz. There has to be a simile for this—
a mercurial "V" of geese, waving

faintly above battened fields of grist,
a "V" that neither alights nor vanishes since,
in doing either, it wouldn't be a "V."

(1945-1967)

My old beau's dead. May God rest
his bashed-in head on a moss pillow,
may his big body rise to intercept a football
again, as a defensive cloud-formation.

Decades are crushed clover, sex
a murmurous echo, the future indistinct
from grass. Rust seasons his name as whiplash,
but why describe a fatal hiking accident

as the last page of the Iliad? He wore
the wrong shoes, and that's that. Sandals
were the end of him on a wet, rock-inclined
afternoon. Had he worn boots, he'd be

in The White House, or in Wisconsin.
He set his sights high, but dressed down
for a waterfall expedition to the outreaches of
Hong Kong. If only stories weren't true.

MOON ROC

Someday we'll meet and shoot the bull.
By then, the rest home will be full.
The shiftless lake will disappear,
as will the rowboat and the deer.

Scalloped ripples, wakes of oars,
the forest picnics with passels of lice,
will be, as an early marriage lost,
insomnia's favorite flight, but

until the city's curfews begin and
double-decked tourists evaporate and
manholes implode and tuskless elephants
immigrate, you are my good night,

my shouldered Magritte, my scripted pipe.
Are all the lights out? Have you checked?

MARVELLIAN MAGIC

Ivy's invasive, it smothers traces
of burly hostas and filigrees of ferns,
then climbs, with Himalayan force, any
fence, its leaves green conquistadors.

My yard's doomed by silent armies,
my trees endangered by alpine cleats,
by slow massive English rigor, sentries
who never sleep. If annihilation is all

that's made, if the green thought in
the green shade is ivy, and oblivion is
weeds subdued, I live in an obliteration
of green, aggressive, conniving, rude,

lowly attributes verdancy assumes,
and I need not mow, I need not prune.

A HISTORY OF GARDEN AESTHETICS

Tiers of verdant structure were once
popular: green snakes coiled in a swanboat
at the edge of the river, but revolutions
prevailed, scales without skins, and

we abandoned Malaysian texture,
stamped batiks, returning only to bow
to reeds from a thatched verandah and speak
kindly to each pulsant thing. The impasse

disrupted the weather. Clouds scolded
one another, as if the sky could be defined
by opinion. Birds flew in opposite directions.
Each sought a definite, dignified tree. The

revolutionaries left in a grand exit. Snakes
didn't. Exits and gates don't appeal to snakes.

THREE WEAK STARS

Black branches script the faint winds
as if the calligrapher's brush were thin
and then splotched the crows in to give
trees hunger, restless revelations.

The soil is drenched weed-pulp,
greening by the minute as if spring
were devouring death in a fast overlap,
a green sprint. The roots' ghosts

are back, cloaked in emeralds, the
daffodils' shrill singular hue enhanced
by umbrellas of cloud: portraiture's props.
The rainy overcast outdoes Photoshop,

saturates the surround. "Three weak stars"
hide in the sky. You put them there to
give the cloud umbrellas an outlet, a
heightening effect for wild color.

RENDEZVOUS

He wanted to tell me something
He had not told anyone before
It might have been anything
When he moved through the door

He had not told anyone before
Unsure of what he wanted to know
When he moved through the door
And took off all his clothes

Unsure of what he wanted to know
Or what he thought true at the time
When he took off all his clothes
And asked me to take off mine

What he thought true at the time
He was careful to keep to himself
When he asked me to take off mine
He watched but he would not help

He was careful to keep to himself
As if asking me to do something
He watched but he would not help
He indicated I knew everything

As if asking me to do something
He had not told anyone before
He indicated I knew everything
When he moved through the door

He had not told anyone before
He wanted to tell me something
When he moved through the door
It might have been anything

Bill Finn - 2010

OCCUPIED

She was his empty room,
the room he never settled into,
but left there like a strand of hair
on an untouched pillow–

an island in the sea beyond
a door he never passed through
for fear of the truth, the missing
postcard of that room,

the no-postcard view. It
was always a space that to him
was unessential, a space he never
claimed to need: a variant

of sleep, a neat mess. He
rose and dressed, wrote and
slept, with no wish for holidays
or an occasional guest.

LOST IN THE FAR-FLOWN STARS

As a mermaid on a pirate's plank slips
off the ship into blue froth, so the child dreams
on a magic pillow to reach the tooth fairy's
realms of frilled radiance with swirling

hems, of quiet-colored fairymen, of hip-
huggers that mix and match, of stand-up violins.
In such dreams, the passion police run out of gas
and every salesman rings every bell, but

transports to fairyland don't always go well.
The hyperbole of doubt takes a seat in the amphitheater
to observe the mysteries deciphered by dust, and
the hymnlike shimmer cools; all that's splendid

turns into mud and the eventide's moonflower
lands with a thud on the bedroom floor and a mermaid
swims to the top of the door to quote a raven.

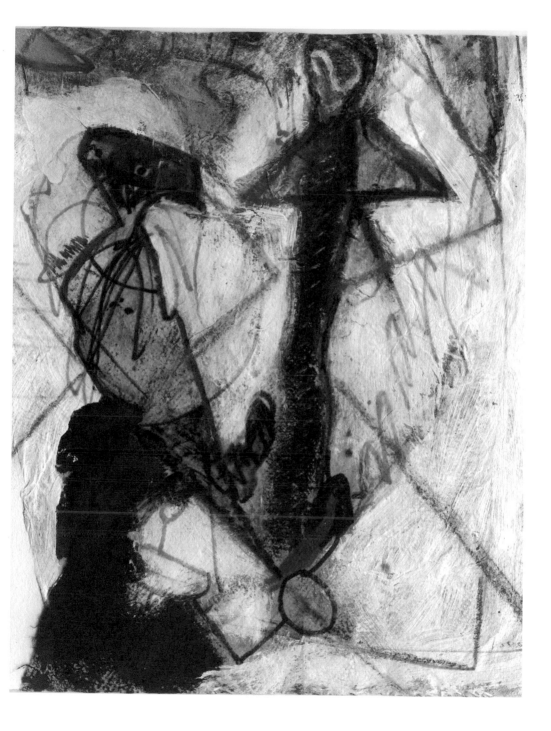

THE NUMEN OF NUMBERS

Thirteen elevators rise in a normal nightmare.
There are thirteen hoofprints on the nearest stair.

Thirteen stains mark each embankment.
A sergeant trains troops for thirteen engagements.

A woman hides her eyes in thirteen evasions.
Every continent's comprised of thirteen nations.

When love is unspoken there are thirteen reasons.
When the dead reassemble there are thirteen conventions.

A tsunami warns the shore in thirteen waves.
A char-a-banc on tour reaches thirteen caves.

A sunset contains thirteen astonishments.
Shattered on the outlands are thirteen monuments.

Thirteen blisters singe one solar stare,
so why is there a blind spot, a blind spot everywhere?

AS ROMANCE FAILS

Indolence fans the aqua pools
before lovers' spats prelude dawn's make-up sex.
A chilling sky ensues, as everyone fears love,
the great mummer of regrets. Yet,

not even trees control their destinies,
half-stilled by burlesque bees, bird-burdened.
Nor can they turn upright one fallen limb, languishing
as if lonesome. You, Richard, have grown,

a green sailor upon a mulched sea, closer
to love, to reality, to the seashells of woodbine,
the seraph's tunes; and, soon, trust,

regret's second cousin, will alarm you
with devotion: its rose-lilting fathoms, their glass eye,
enfold bold ecrivians who, far-flung, revive.

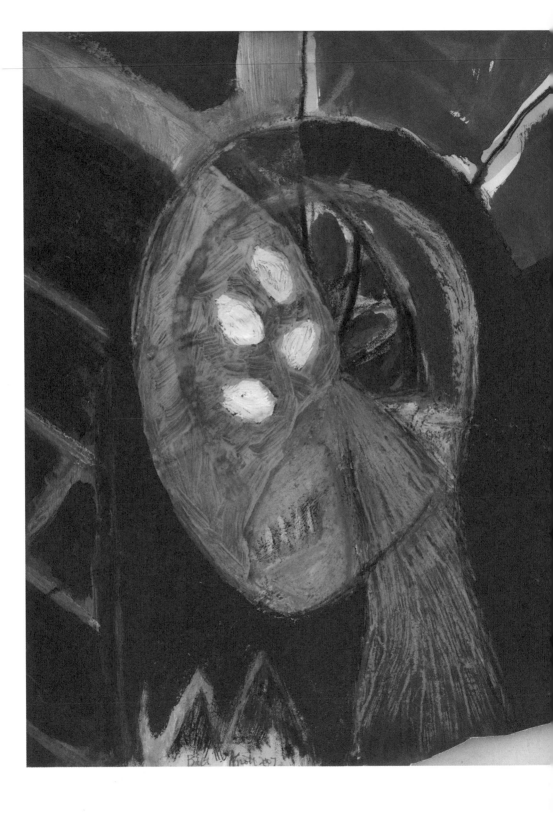

WELL-ROUNDED

Topiaries of sea turtles vanish
like a flea market in the clarity of dawn.
The barking of a dog seems parochial,
a trellis in the fog. We were

the bulkhead of a double bed
but we didn't last long; the ceiling
had the overall feeling of the Hindenburg,
a combustion of dreams indicted

by state troopers. They disappeared
like fireflies under a parachute and now
dawn's clarity is a clock, a wise orb.
We no longer have the need to be

phosphorescent about the break-up
or the twig-snipped turtles we so loved.
They, like a house in the ocean, were ours.

THE NEAREST SPRAIN

By replacing "you" with another "you"–
the one "you" a tumulus, the other a river
of inkfish under dark trees intermeshed
in a mysterious feud–I could alter

the towpath, its circuitous views,
but such a tactic is overcharged, so I
prefer hanging out in warm outpourings,
liquid vestibules, where I feel feverish,

but not too. I drop my "you"s
and dream of Napoleon's letters home.
A cluster of locusts passes. Their drone
is like the end of surrealism again.

The brushfires are laughing. I guess
the towpath is a julep, a swallowed glass,
my unicycle busted, and "you" and "you"
are powder, a blunderbuss of facts.

YEARS OF YEARS

The laden hastiness of "yes"–
as if no other accommodation were
available and the bus just passed
moments ago into mystic dust,

one's last lover waving from a
vanishing window after promising
to call you–this must be the "yes"
of lust. How many times did I

do what I really didn't want to?
A gazillion. They call it The Too-
June Syndrome. Some believe there
are twelve Junes and that's it,

but, when age sets in, the entire
calendar consumes you, concentrating
upon late October, when lust, light
and "yes" wave from an even

slower bus window and the lover
who disappeared, whom you forgot,
who forgot you, calls to say hi.

SUBVERSION

Under the rain, its kaftans of faces,
above the butterweed of similar places,
between the cabin and the cantata,
are thin aerial arrays.

Amid their traces, pillaged by bees,
lurk the lidded laboratories
with their Vitria of capsulated eyes
and persona grata discoveries...

There is, however, moonlight
on the ever-postmorteming frieze,
dashes of plashed peppergrass

moistening the flagrante delictos—
a more abstruse, deranging vision
of fallibility or in uteros of love.

SHOWDOWN

I fell in love with a non-existent idea,
a similitude undermining the window. I
took your hand. You showed me nowhere.
Now yesterday's spaghetti sauce is gone.

Your circle of plans sets aside what I
always presumed I could never neglect–
the there and where of the stair and chair–
and I suspect my ossified views pass

as true, but you never look at them,
do you? You cast impossibility back to me
as if you were prologue only, a prompter,
and now I'm the window's quandary,

a towhead with a thought. You've
incrementally abandoned me. I hate irony.
I like the selfless quiet that surrounds me.

WAKEFUL

We don't understand admirable
reversals that make the dress code an
Adirondack chair, nor do we recognize
that wallpaper is plausible, patterned
et ceteras of apples and pears.

We dwell in a house that could be
anywhere at four in the morning when
the night is dark and vivid as a gracious
umbrella and bodhisattvas descend
to remind us of the weather which

is more mild than summer's shine.
Time wears slippers on islands of time
above the napping desk. Doorways rest
like tipped-over boats in a soft ocean
where every casualty is saved

in a collage of commotion. Only
love makes sense as the years pirouette
and hum a tune that always ends with
"Back to you, John, back to you."

NUANCE

Less faraway than gay, something
encloses me, some somber sexuality
evangelic in origin, not exactly an orgy,
but more a circulation, coupled

by vampire abstinence, hesitation,
inswirled intimacy that seldom happens.
Do you think I need surgery? Or will
beet juice do? I am evolving. My

neck is teething, touched. My breath
has had enough breath, yet isn't ceasing.
I'm in a spell-in-the-stairwell sort of feeling,
wan, urgent, spiral, and you aren't

moving, just touching, and the drapes
are velvet, fuzzed maroon, and the room
is expiring like a tired roach, a roach
that's seen everything evident.

RESOLVE

Lately it's been late in the day,
the lavish firmament grey as a whisper
in a living room bathed in blood. Winters
have unspooled from a missing sun

like a silk thread under a guillotine.
The daisies are goblin-faced, but without
surprise. The brain needs to either shave or
to compromise, to lift off, like a water

turkey, from the streaming dream. I
like you best when you stroll away from
my latest scene telling me to drink less Splenda,
then splash the sidewalk with

cherry bombs: that gesture wakes up
the nonexistent, the strewn corpses on the
L-shaped couch awaiting the coroner's report.
I dustbin dementia pretty quick when you go out.

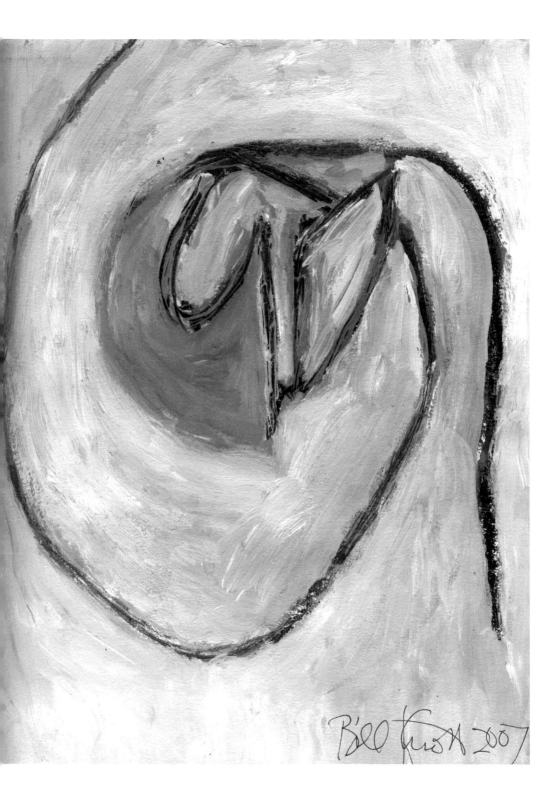

DEEP DENIM

We both probably own too much property.
We could shed some snow. The windowpanes
are short of breath. Girls with long braids
who steal souls have left the night shift

and the seagull tavern's dartboard is bereft;
the happy hour is empty, like on-tap dread. We
need more names for answers we can't give,
for abstract uncertainty. The lagoon is

in a telephone booth we no longer use;
it used to be too fat to fit but an all-around
slendering has set in, a slendering that drips.
I've had enough of uncollectible trinkets

that make me frantically unwed. Society
has pierced my ears and the latitudes are now
incorporated, like three-piece clouds. Vistas are
musty or too loud; you don't wear a suit?

THE MOMENT'S DELTA

A miniature red Japanese maple, its
branches splayed like a waist-high bonsai,
reminds me of the Gates-Crowley controversy
until I return to your summoning flume

where news is ideation and overly legible
like large-type on The Big Island, a billboard
amidst the pineapple plantations that switched
to cannabis production in the mid-sixties

when everyone on the road appeared as
a reborn Jesus freak in the midst of a bee swarm.
My attitudes resist compassion. I've learned
nothing from the banyan, its huge shade.

My rain, my city, is man-made unlike
the stunted maple, a summer garden trophy;
its red leaves, offsetting sexually-suggestive
irises and burst bulbs, undermine me.

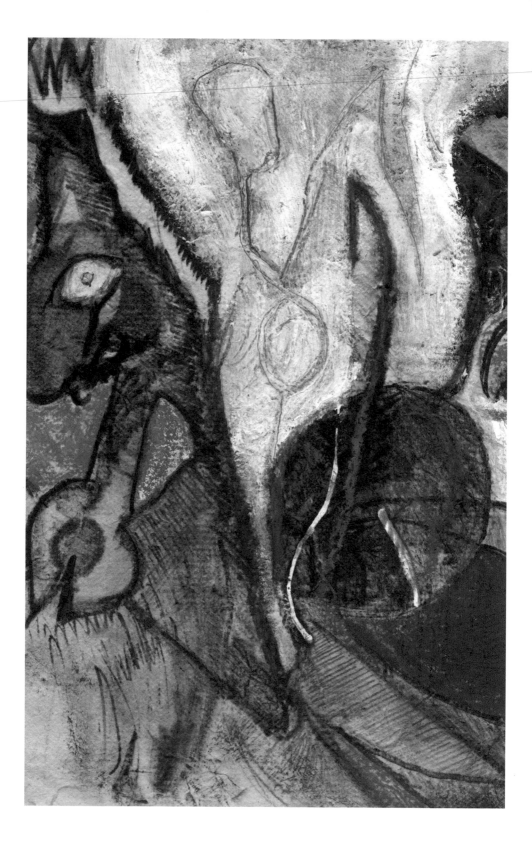

RISIBLE

Bloated thunder, its thick beard
of nervous trees, rustles the burrs
that enliven me, my pale-purple thistles
a vased oddity of spiny poufs.

Rain erupts and the future goes
blank. I stare from a fish tank of soon.
You like to deliberate and soothe as if you
were a mortician counting decibels

to limn water's recesses, should
the coffin sink. The storm has departed
within a blink but it made the horizon stop.
Lines are fine sometimes but not a lot.

I like thumbtacks on balsa. I wonder
what Oprah thinks of the rain's delirium
and if Dr. Phil will weigh in. No, I don't.

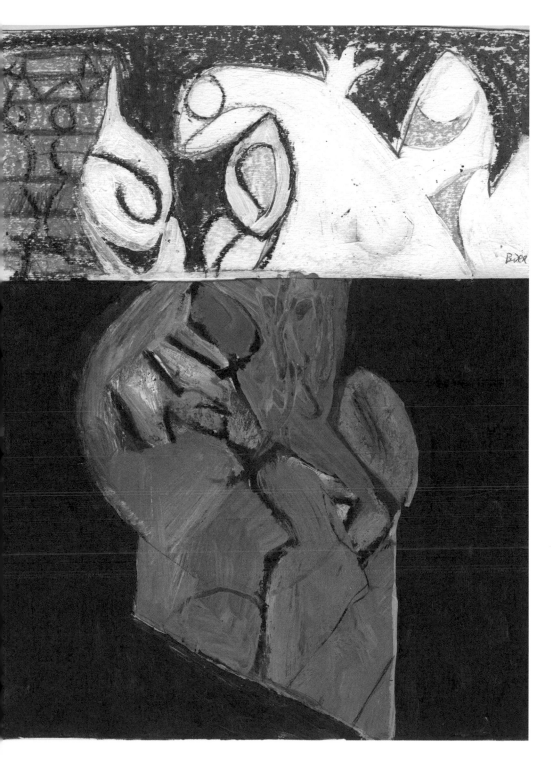

MORE MIX-UPS

What do we mean when we mean
to be clear? Are all pebbles seemingly
organized? Is the spider web a shadow
of floating horsehair, the ragged

shrub a fountain of sound? I was
beginning to unbraid dimness sideways
when your aura of snipped beginnings
re-arrived and I slowed down

to take in the remote travel inns,
their balconies of wisteria, but I've
become a shallow tumble as facile as
forsythia is yellow, but is it yellow

all the time? Are doubts polygamous
bedfellows, old Joseph Smith Jr. cartoons?
Are feelings dead, or do we err and
amble to amble and err again?

MINDREADER

My sash got caught in the near-dark
of high noon, a flipflop's plan gone awry.
Considering the topheavy imperium that makes
a madhouse clairvoyant, there's an argument

for aging. Like a stopwatch dropped
from the lowest berth on a yacht, nothing
slips by without feigning time, without clocking
a flounder, or visualizing Pensacola,

its fronded harmonies, the frondeur's
fronds. You are my hip replacement, my
corrective laser; you're the aneurysm that never
arrives, the twilight of late parties, the

dance floor that let's them be. You silver
all occasions with silvered sanity until the sash
is unsnared and flipflops to earlier parties.

SWITCHWORK

The day is a non-throwaway,
the hour a ruby, the locale perishable.
Is this the setting you meant by "spring?"
Is vision reliable? Or is it a headtrip

that needs a walk? Ah, spring,
hopscotch chalk, it is now October.
Stray trimmings fall like clipped whiskers.
They are claimants rather than obstacles.

They want everything terrible
moved out of the way. They like
the provident and the unattired. I'd talk
about it but I'm leaving. I've assumed

a personality and that's bad.
My spirit medium is in the shower,
and you're everything I've ever had.

THE FIRE'S FLIGHT

I'd be kinder in a kitchen, but I've
been ruined by competition, by my own
driven situation, by caulked nerves. Now,
December's the final word. The guy I
chose is the wrong guy, the cosmos

is absurd, I tread the pavements and
sank below the earth like a docked fan. I
made too much of you, as only the lonely
understand before they grow up. If you

weren't from California I wouldn't
have given you a second look, but you're
a transport, a refugee from the valley, all sun,
no sea, and, as a refugee from Hawaii, I'm

intrigued. Should have known, should have
known, or did I use you to remain free? Did I
buy an entire hotel to preserve one dream?

THE BUNGLER'S CREW

Only the military grinds you down
or grinds you into the ground, either way.
Its kids are bratty, they like to say, whereas
I, I am a boat of teeth, a few minutes

of comedy in a solarium at midnight
with an audience of one: a jade plant. I
seek lesser concepts: a lake dematerializing
into snap turtles with diesel propellers

ten feet away. I camouflage the inevitable.
The sky's a drop-shot, at last. An osprey makes
an overpass. I don't exist. I swim within rims
of crumpled fish-bait trash, a prey, a soup,

an exoskeleton. I'm left behind when
work needs to be done, work no one wants
to do unless they believe in you, my country.
Thinking never was your top priority.

CRATERED

I know you've been inducted
onto the carousel, its skeins of pigtails,
its melon-colored steeds, its cancan music
that swirls as a Ferris wheel in a flask,

but have you hidden any details,
any sullen elsewheres blocking the path?
Have you been casual and coy rather
than wrathful, in need of a bath?

I have, but fallen pennies own
their wishes so I thought I'd ask, now
that winter is no longer a spa or a tricycle
dropped from the sky. Are you,

like me, unable to cry? Do your
divinations need companions? I would,
but cannot, take your hand. We'll just stare
at bandoleers together, their giant pockets.

ODE TO RADNITZKY

I can't be a celebrity
because I punctuate. I dig
up arrowheads for exclamation
points, then make the mistake

of believing repetition can
be renewed, as if sculpture were
a wiry mobile of coat hangers Man
Ray didn't do ninety years ago

when he was in art school.
Pass the gravel and make it cool.
I like mine grey. The road is too
possible. It's in the way. I'm

Thumbelina on a pterosaur,
valleys a groan of tangled trees.
This ride was done in the movies,
movies Man Ray's already seen.

UNCLE ELWOOD'S NIECE

The room entered me and, ever since,
whenever I meet someone for cappuccino
on Sunday, I'm asked if my sofa is blue
and, if so, do I have an oval room,

and, if I do, is the mantel wood? So
I prefer a different take on orchids; that
of a lemming on a ladder to heaven. My
room has no picture-hangers; its walls

are hapless. In the modesty of autumn,
I'll do repairs. How are the false excuses
over there? Is the gridlock novelizing
and, if so, do the trucks gleam? Is

the situation a clinched situation
or only the way jump-starting seems?
And I wonder what clarities we haven't
mentioned, and if the ladder has rungs?

Has the caregiver come, the clock-
stopper? You've push-pinned the index
cards into plots. We're set to endeavor,
we own no co-op, we're existential,

yet the top hat seems like a body sock,
soft as sable, and there're no beams.

LEADED

Wives want to be what they aren't usually.
My mother got fed up with the questionable
deal; she wanted maids and private clubs
where any sex could swim in the pool.

She did whatever she wanted and sent
us to school. She loved everything but
housework. My father flew and flew; the
War College wanted him to. His career

was taking orders. Orders were the rule.
You die for orders after being trained to do
what abuses you. Metal helps but it doesn't
protect you. I metal my selfishness, my

urban I-don't-know. My Golden Rule
is corroded by opiates, the home-team flag
triangulated by hidden coffins, business tips,
state-dinner party-crashers, publicity, hype,

until nothing seen beyond four blocks
is relevant, until what is immediate is slight.

"TO BECOME WHAT ONE IS"

The cottage dissolves, its serenity lost
in the distribution of sidewalks. You rise
to greet a tollbooth at the front door. The
placid brook gives way to a less sylvan

allure: a doctor's appointment, a game
plan, a pre-scheduled handshake. You long
for a porch in the woods, for bunched flowers
in a blue bottle, but the guest-free sanctity

is gone. A five-hour echo of nostalgia,
its blown fuse, takes over. A lockstep greets
the asphalt's near future. But you are neither
here nor there, my samovar, my incidental

pleasure. You're a lowly stratosphere, your
wardrobe the weather. Look, I say, climbing
up the domed observatory's tower, it's dark.

LOST SPROCKET

Time is elusive, as if it dropped a breeze down
a canister, then shook it. The rattlesnake séance
with its unusual hymn is like a salt marsh

filled with millenniums, dalliance embroiled.
Good morning, the past is forgiven. I'm stepping
back like a scythe from a reed, humbly. I'm avoiding
excursions while I can. I'm not free. I shun sailing,

my journal a bedspread too tucked-in, my heart
a bookmark on a white page. I steep black tea with
a jinn. I can no longer open a window screen or
salvage a centenarian tree or breathe within

the iron maiden of fantasy or read of massacres
or clearly see. Clouds scratch their backs above me.

BRIDGED BY EAVES

Ceravolo, it snows. The sky
is cotton-cold and unseeming.
I bathe to wash away non-feeling.
The rice of daylight

whitens the roofs until
civilized streets are brambles
on Wang Wei screens–

mists adrift above rose-pink mountains.

Ceravolo, fresh snow on wet slate,
long ago is just a sec; no gift is late.